Worker Bees

by Kristin Cashore

PEARSON

Scott
Foresman

Editorial Offices: Glenview, Illinois • Parsippany, New Jersey • New York, New York
Sales Offices: Needham, Massachusetts • Duluth, Georgia • Glenview, Illinois
Coppell, Texas • Sacramento, California • Mesa, Arizona

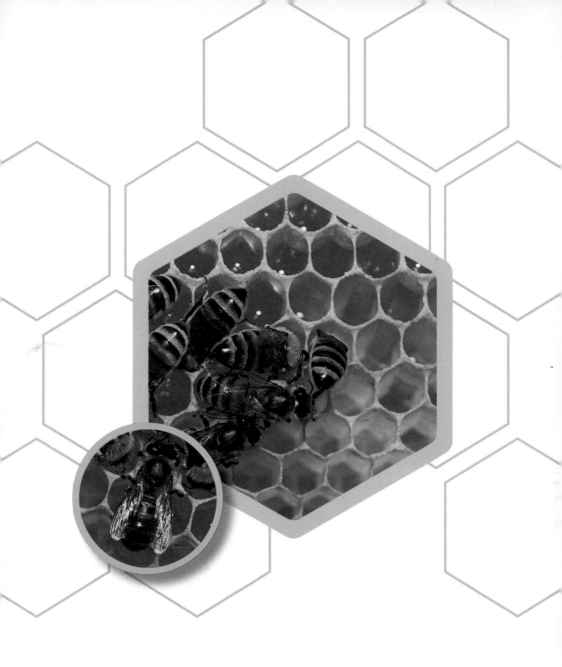

Worker bees help their family.
They keep the hive working.

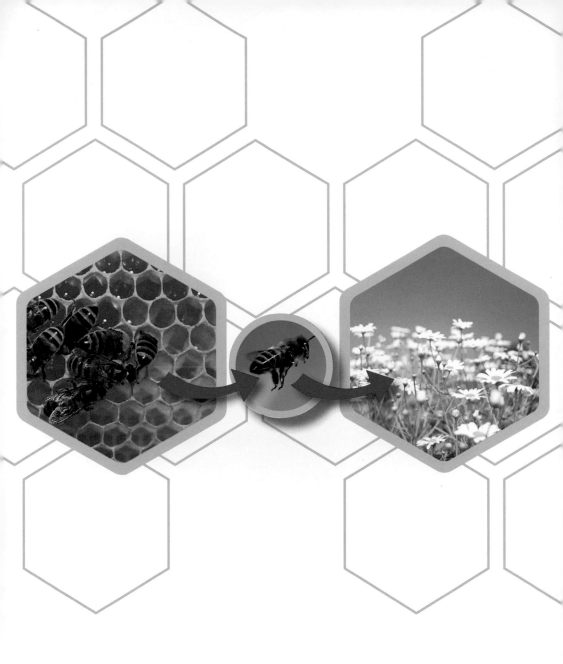

Worker bees help their family.

Some bees fly to flowers.

Worker bees help their family.
Some bees get nectar and pollen.

Worker bees help their family.
Some bees use nectar
to make honey.

Worker bees help their family.
Other bees use pollen
to feed new bees.

Worker bees help their family.
They also help us!